STEAM IN THE NORTH WEST

Fred Kerr

PEN & SWORD
TRANSPORT

First published in Great Britain in 2018 by
Pen & Sword Transport
An imprint of
Pen & Sword Books Ltd
47 Church Street
Barnsley
South Yorkshire
S70 2AS

ISBN 978 1 52671 745 0

A CIP catalogue record for this book is
available from the British Library.

Typeset in 11pt Minion by Mac Style Ltd, Bridlington, East Yorkshire
Printed and bound in India by Replika Press Pvt Ltd

Pen & Sword Books Limited incorporates the imprints of Atlas, Archaeology, Aviation, Discovery, Family History,
Fiction, History, Maritime, Military, Military Classics, Politics, Select, Transport, True Crime, Air World,
Frontline Publishing, Leo Cooper, Remember When, Seaforth Publishing, The Praetorian Press,
Wharncliffe Local History, Wharncliffe Transport, Wharncliffe True Crime and White Owl.

For a complete list of Pen & Sword titles please contact
PEN & SWORD BOOKS LIMITED
47 Church Street, Barnsley, South Yorkshire, S70 2AS, England
E-mail: enquiries@pen-and-sword.co.uk
Website: www.pen-and-sword.co.uk

Front Cover: Stanier 'Royal Scot' Class 4-6-0 46115 *Scots Guardsman* curves through Helwith Bridge on 7 February 2009 whilst working the Hellifield–Carlisle leg of a Manchester Victoria–Carlisle railtour.

Rear Cover: 44767 *George Stephenson*, with Stephenson valve gear, climbs through Giggleswick on 31 March 1984 whilst working the Hellifield–Carnforth leg of a southbound CUMBRIAN MOUNTAIN EXPRESS returning from Carlisle to Euston.

Contents

It is generally accepted that Britain's railway network originated in 1825 with the opening of the Stockton & Darlington Railway. This line was built to transport coal from local mines and the carriage of passengers was an unexpected, but bonus, traffic. The first railway line that was specifically designed to carry passengers was the Liverpool & Manchester Railway that opened in 1830. Not only did this railway carry both passenger and freight traffic between the industrial centres of Liverpool and Manchester, but it also established a relationship between the North West of England and steam locomotives.

It was a relationship that lasted until August 1968, when the region saw the final operation of steam locomotives on British Railways (BR) that was formally ended on 11 August 1968 by the running of a special train from Liverpool. The train was identified as '1T57' (its train reporting number) but is more commonly known by its nickname of 'The Fifteen Guinea Special' (the price of a ticket) as it ran from Liverpool Lime Street to Carlisle via Manchester Victoria, Bolton, Blackburn, Hellifield and the Settle & Carlisle (S&C) route. The train was operated in stages during the day and used five locomotives: Stanier Class 5 4-6-0s 44781, 44871, 45110 and 45305 and Standard Class 7 'Britannia' 4-6-2 70013 *Oliver Cromwell*.

There was an exception to this cessation of steam operation in the guise of Gresley 'A3' Class 4-6-2 4472/60103 *Flying Scotsman* which was privately owned, and whose owner had negotiated a contract with BR that continued until 1969. Apart from this locomotive, all other steam locomotive operations were henceforth to be confined to preserved/heritage lines only.

The first signs of change came in 1971 when BR allowed the trial running of 'King' Class 4-6-0 6000 *King George V* which proved sufficiently successful that, from June 1972, steam traction was permitted to haul charter/railtour trains on a limited number of secondary main lines. The list of approved lines was slowly increased until 1994, when the privatisation of BR included a policy of 'Open Access' that granted steam locomotives the right to operate on the privatised network, subject to meeting certain conditions and weight and gauge restrictions.

The consequence in the North West of England was the opportunity to operate steam-hauled trains over the two major climbs within the region – the Settle–Carlisle route (S&C) with its lengthy climb from Settle to Ais Gill (known as 'the Long Drag') and the West Coast Main Line (WCML) route over Shap where locomotive performance could be tested to the full. The main pool of locomotives comprised of preserved examples that had originally been operated by the 'local' London Midland Region (LMR) of BR but, over time, preserved locomotives from BR's three other regions also made occasional visits.

This album seeks to show the wide variety of locomotives that have operated within the North West of England since the easing of restrictions began in 1972, noting that the 'North West' has been defined as that area north of Crewe to Carlisle, east of Crewe to the Calder Valley at Hall Royd Junction (Todmorden), south in the Peak District to Buxton and an eastern boundary formed by the S&C route between Hellifield and Carlisle. While the locomotives classes of each region are shown in order of their BR fleet numbers, note that some locomotives have operated with an earlier (pre-BR) fleet number as allocated by their post-Grouping operating company; irrespective of their running number, locomotive classes are shown in their BR fleet numbering sequence.

@ Fred Kerr March 2018

Black 5 44871 pilots Red 'Jubilee' Class 5 4-6-0 5690 *Leander* through Dove Holes on 26 February 2011 whilst en route to Buxton with a Lancaster–Buxton railtour.

Section 1:
London Midland Region (LMR)

On 1 January 1923 the Transport Act 1922 became effective and grouped the railway network of the day into four separate companies, with companies in the North West of England becoming part of the London Midland Scottish Railway (LMSR). This grouping of railway companies included the Lancashire & Yorkshire Railway (LYR) with its workshops at Horwich, the London North Western Railway (LNWR) with its workshops at Crewe and the Midland Railway (MR) with its workshops at Derby and these, plus many minor railway companies, were melded over time into the one company as LMSR.

On 1 January 1948, when the railways were nationalised under the Transport Act 1947, the four Grouping companies became regions of the new British Railways with the LMSR then becoming British Railways London Midland Region (BR(LMR)) and its locomotive fleet adding 40000 to its fleet numbers as a result.

DEELEY CLASS 4P 4-4-0
BR = 41000–41044

This class was designed by Johnson and introduced in 1902 then rebuilt by Fowler from 1914 with superheater, whilst (4)1000–(4)1004 were introduced by Deeley in 1905, as a development of the Johnson design, that was subsequently fitted with superheater. MR 1000 (BR = 41000) joined the National Collection when withdrawn from service in 1959 and was restored to running order in its 1914 MR condition. It formed part of the stock transferred to the National Rail Museum at York in 1977 from where it continued to operate on the main line. When withdrawn from service in the 1980s it became a display item that has since visited various heritage lines representing the NRM.

One of the last runs of MR 1000 was on 28 September 1983 when it powered a York–Rochdale charter on behalf of the NRM; it is here seen climbing the approach to Hebden Bridge on its outward journey.

STANIER CLASS 6P5F 2-6-0
BR = 42945–42984

This class was the first locomotive design from William Stanier following his arrival from Swindon as Chief Mechanical Engineer in 1932 and was created as an improvement to the Hughes/Fowler design of 42700–42944. The improvements included such features as a taper boiler and other features that were common practice within the Swindon workshops of the Great Western Railway.

42968 was the penultimate class member to be withdrawn in December 1966, and was rescued from Barry Scrapyard in December 1973 to enter preservation with the Severn Valley Railway, where it is currently based as at December 2016. In December 1996 it made a rare return to main line operation when it worked the Crewe–Carlisle leg of a charter from Hitchin to Carlisle. The train is noted heading north through Winwick on 21 December 1996 with the locomotive bearing LMSR fleet number and Black livery with Red Lining.

STANIER CLASS 5MT 4-6-0
BR = 44658–45499

This class of 842 locomotives was introduced by William Stanier in 1934 for mixed traffic duties, and construction continued until the appearance of 44697 as the final locomotive of the class when released from Horwich Works in December 1950. Construction had begun from (4)5000 but when the number series reached (4)5499, subsequent batch orders were numbered backwards from (4)4999. Some of these later batches were trialled with a variety of modifications such as the fitting of roller bearings, use of Caprotti valve gear, fitting of Stephenson link motion, steel firebox and combinations of the modifications.

The design was the LMSR equivalent of the GWR 'Hall' class of locomotives and class members quickly demonstrated an ability to handle trains from the lowliest trip working to the fastest expresses. During the final years of steam operation on BR services, this ability was tested to the limit as reliable steam locomotives became harder to find when locomotives were withdrawn for the least excuse to make way for the new build of replacement diesel and electric locomotives.

Eighteen locomotives have been preserved, including six rescued from Barry Scrapyard, and they have proved an excellent source of power for many nascent heritage lines but, once main line running was restored, their operating abilities quickly came to the fore and, during the first decade of the twenty-first century, class members have re-established the reputation of the class for reliable and powerful traction.

Left: 44871 pilots 45407 *The Lancashire Fusilier* through Oubeck curve on 28 January 2012 as they prepare for a water stop at Carnforth whilst working the outward leg of a Manchester Victoria–Carlisle charter.

Right: 44932, the first of the class to be built by Horwich Works, pilots 45305 out of Carnforth Goods Loop on 18 February 2012 after replacing Class 86/2 86259 *Les Ross* on the outward leg of a Euston–Carlisle railtour.

Left: 45407 accelerates through Clitheroe on 25 October 2008 with the outward leg of a Manchester Victoria–Carlisle railtour.

Below Left: 45407 *The Lancashire Fusilier* accelerates through Clitheroe on 30 June 2007 with the outward leg of a Manchester Victoria–Carlisle railtour.

Below Right: 45407, in the guise of 45157 *The Glasgow Highlander*, pilots 'Royal' Class 47/7 47798 *Prince William* through Leyland on 3 June 2002 whilst working the outward leg of a Manchester Victoria–Carlisle railtour via the Ribble Valley and S&C route.

Opposite page

Left: Black 5 44871 pilots Red 'Jubilee' Class 5 4-6-0 5690 *Leander* through Dove Holes on 26 February 2011 whilst en route to Buxton with a Lancaster–Buxton railtour which

Right: returned via Peak Forest where the duo passed Class 66/4 66431 which had just arrived with its train.

45110, one of the locomotives used on the 1968 '15 Guinea Special', is based on the Severn Valley Railway but, on 23 October 1999, it made a rare appearance on the main line when it pilotted 45407 on a Crewe–Carlisle railtour, here seen passing Oubeck on the northbound journey.

45305, bearing LMSR Unlined Black livery and fleet number, climbs out of Settle on 25 November 1989 whilst working a Euston–Carlisle railtour.

44767 *George Stephenson*, with Stephenson valve gear, climbs through Giggleswick on 31 March 1984 whilst working the Hellifield–Carnforth leg of a southbound CUMBRIAN MOUNTAIN EXPRESS returning from Carlisle to Euston.

45407 *The Lancashire Fusilier* pulls out of Blackpool North on 22 July 2000 with a Blackpool North–Carlisle charter, organised by Preston local transport operator John Fishwick to celebrate the company's centenary.

44871 pilots 45407 *The Lancashire Fusilier* through the northern fells at Greenholme on 28 January 2012 whilst working a Manchester Victoria–Carlisle railtour.

44932, the first of the class built by Horwich Works, climbs out of Meols Cop on 3 November 1985 whilst working a Southport–Manchester Victoria charter during a day of steam tours organised by the local *Southport Visitor* newspaper and the Liverpool Area Manager's office.

44871 pilots 45407 *The Lancashire Fusilier* through the northern fells at Greenholme on 30 December 2009 whilst working a Manchester Victoria–Carlisle railtour.

Hard to believe but those two photographs were taken on the same day – and only a few miles apart.

Left: 45407 *The Lancashire Fusilier* pilots Standard Class 4 2-6-0 76079 on 4 March 2006 as they drift along the Blackburn–Bolton direct line at Chapeltown, whilst working a circular railtour from Liverpool Lime St, after stopping at Blackburn for a planned water stop.

Below: Only two hours earlier the duo had reached the summit of Copy Pit on the Todmorden–Blackburn line where snow lay deep on the exposed hillside.

Opposite Page

Above: 44871 pilots 45407 *The Lancashire Fusilier* as the duo power off Ribblehead Viaduct on 28 January 2012 whilst working a railtour returning from Carlisle to Manchester Victoria.

Below: 45407 *The Lancashire Fusilier* pilots Standard Class 4 2-6-0 76079 as they climb through Selside on 20 December 2005 whilst working the Hellifield–Carlisle leg of a Bedford–Carlisle railtour.

For a short period during 2004/5, 45407 carried the identity of sister locomotive 44996 with the embellishments of the Scotland-based locomotive that included larger numerals.

Left: 45407 pilots Standard Class 4 2-6-0 76079 through Peak Forest on 22 October 2005 whilst working a railtour returning from Buxton to Euston.

Below: 45407 stands at Preston on 26 October 2005 whilst working a Blackpool Illuminations special returning from Blackpool North to Rawtenstall on the East Lancashire Railway.

45407 curves through Greenholme on 30 October 2004 whilst ascending Shap with a Manchester Victoria–Carlisle railtour.

Above: 45231 *The Sherwood Forester* accelerates past Lostock Hall on 12 August 2015 whilst working the weekly FELLSMAN railtour from Lancaster to Carlisle via the S&C route.

Left: 45231 *The Sherwood Forester* approaches Lostock Hall on 27 August 2014 whilst working the weekly FELLSMAN railtour from Lancaster to Carlisle via the S&C route.

Below: 45305 climbs through Euxton on 6 August 2011 whilst working the return CUMBRIAN MOUNTAIN EXPRESS railtour from Carlisle to Liverpool Lime St.

45305 breasts Hoghton Summit on 4 February 2011 with the Preston–Carlisle leg of the CUMBRIAN MOUNTAIN EXPRESS railtour from Euston to Carlisle routed via the S&C.

Above: 45407, in the guise of 45157 *The Glasgow Highlander* passes Shaw & Crompton on 15 September 2002 with one of a series of railtours running that day from Manchester Victoria to Manchester Victoria via the Oldham Loop.

Opposite page

Left: 45407 *The Lancashire Fusilier* is pilotted by 44871 as they wait to depart from Preston on 1 November 2015 with THE TIN BATH circular railtour to Sheffield via Manchester and the Hope Valley that returned via Huddersfield.

Right: The duo join the main line at New Mills Junction after passing through Romiley where a stop had been made for water.

STANIER 'JUBILEE' CLASS 4-6-0
BR = 45552–45742

This class of 191 locomotives was introduced by Sir William Stanier in 1935 as a development of (Sir) Henry Fowler's 'Patriot' class, to work secondary express services that they did extensively throughout the LMSR system. The class was initially designated as 5XP (Express Passenger) and delivered in LMSR Red livery hence their being described as 'Red 5' to distinguish them from the 'Black 5' designation of his earlier mixed traffic design.

In the BR era, class members were painted in lined Brunswick Green and the last withdrawal from service took place in late 1967 following which two class members, 45593 *Kolhapur* and 45596 *Bahamas*, entered preservation with private owners. The most interesting return to main line action, however, is that of 45690 *Leander*/45699 *Galatea* which were withdrawn from service in 1964 and sold to Dai Woodham for scrapping at his Barry scrapyard. This pair was among the many locomotives rescued for preservation and, as at December 2016, both see regular use on the main line.

45596 *Bahamas* makes a rare main line appearance away from its base on the Keighley & Worth Valley Railway on 28 June 1992 when the railway ran a charter train from Keighley to Carlisle to celebrate the 125th anniversary of its line opening. The charter is seen on its approach to Garsdale where a stop was made to take on water.

Above Left: 45690 *Leander*, bearing LMSR Lined Red livery and fleet number, storms through Saltney Junction on 28 January 1984 as it departs from Chester with the Chester–Hereford leg of the WELSH MARCHES EXPRESS.

Above Right: 45593 *Kolhapur*, bearing LMSR Lined Red livery and fleet number, powers through Hoscar on 14 September 1986 with a Wigan Wallgate–Southport railtour during a day of steam tours organised by the local *Southport Visitor* newspaper and the Liverpool Area Manager's office.

Left: 45593 *Kolhapur*, bearing LMSR Lined Red livery and fleet number, climbs through Peak Forest on 25 April 1987 whilst working a return railtour from Buxton to Derby.

45690 *Leander*, bearing LMSR Lined Red livery and fleet number, climbs out of Settle on 19 August 2009 with the seasonal FELLSMAN (Lancaster–Carlisle) service.

Left: 45690 *Leander*, bearing LMSR Lined Red livery and fleet number, breasts Hoghton Summit on 19 August 2009 with the seasonal FELLSMAN (Lancaster–Carlisle) service.

Below: 45690 *Leander*, bearing LMSR Lined Red livery and fleet number, climbs up to Leyland on 29 August 2005 with a charter returning from Blackpool North to Nuneaton.

Right: 45690 *Leander*, bearing LMSR Lined Red livery and fleet number, climbs through Little Strickland on 17 October 2009 whilst working the Carlisle–Carnforth leg of a railtour returning from Carlisle to Tyseley.

Below Left: 45690 *Leander*, bearing BR Lined Black livery, climbs through Euxton on 28 March 2015 whilst working the Preston–Shrewsbury leg of a Bishop Auckland–Shrewsbury charter.

Below Right: 45593 *Kolhapur*, bearing LMSR Lined Red livery and fleet number, approaches Burscough Bridge on 14 September 1986 with a Manchester Victoria–Southport charter during a day of steam tours organised by the local *Southport Visitor* newspaper in association with the Liverpool Area Manager's office.

45596 *Bahamas* curves through Pool Hey on 17 September 1989 with a Manchester Victoria–Southport charter during a day of steam tours organised by the local *Southport Visitor* newspaper in association with the Liverpool Area Manager's office.

The FELLSMAN is a seasonal service that operates from Lancaster to Carlisle via Preston and Hellifield before heading north over the S&C route to Carlisle.

Right: 45690 *Leander*, bearing LMSR Lined Red livery and fleet number, breasts Hoghton Summit on 29 July 2009 with the first run of what was to become a regular seasonal service.

Below Left: 45699 *Galatea* climbs through Langho on 18 June 2014 with the FELLSMAN returning from Carlisle to Lancaster.

Below Right: 45690 *Leander*, bearing LMSR Lined Red livery and fleet number, storms through Brock on 29 July 2009 with the first run of what was to become a regular seasonal service.

45699 *Galatea* powers out of Carnforth Goods Loop on 17 February 2016 whilst working the Carnforth–Carlisle leg of a Coventry–Carlisle charter.

STANIER 'ROYAL SCOT' CLASS 4-6-0
BR = 46100–46170

This class was introduced in 1927 to a design by Sir Henry Fowler that was contracted to the North British Locomotive Company in Glasgow to build, with an initial order for fifty locomotives; a further twenty locomotives were ordered from Derby Works in 1930. The locomotives were designed to work the heaviest express services on the West Coast Main Line, which they achieved until replaced by Sir William Stanier's later Pacific designs.

By the early 1940s, Stanier's policy of standardisation had led to the design of a new boiler to be fitted to the LMSR's fleet of 'Patriot', 'Jubilee' and 'Royal Scot' locomotives. The new design was first trialled on 'Jubilee' Class 4-6-0s 5735 *Comet* and 5736 *Phoenix* and, shortly before his secondment to the War Department, he authorised the conversion of ten 'Royal Scot' locomotives.

Two members of the class have passed into preservation – class doyen 46100 *Royal Scot* and 46115 *Scots Guardsman*.

46100 was sold to Billy Butlin's Holiday Camps as a display item at Skegness when withdrawn from service in October 1962 but sold onto Bressingham Steam Museum in March 1971 from where it was passed through a number of owners until bought by Jeremy Hosking in 2009 and moved to his base at Crewe. Although based in Crewe, the locomotive's only appearance in the North West Region, as at December 2016, has been during December 2015 when it undertook a loaded test run over the Carnforth Circuit to gain main line accreditation, after which the locomotive has worked charter trains along the North Wales Coast and visited heritage lines outside the region.

Following withdrawal from service in December 1965, 46115 also passed through several owners, including a brief spell on the main line in 1978, until sold in 2006 to David Smith, owner of West Coast Railway Company (WCRC), who restored it to working order and it is now based in the region at WCRC's Carnforth base.

Before a locomotive can operate on the main line it must undergo a loaded test run which, in the North West of England, is operated from Carnforth and runs via Hellifield, Blackburn and Preston with a stop at Hellifield being used to closely examine the 'test' locomotive. Both locomotives were tested on this working.

46100 *Royal Scot* was tested on 23 December 2015 and was replete in full BR Brunswick Green livery as it climbed through Longpreston on its approach to Hellifield; following certification 46100 *Royal Scot* returned to its base at Crewe.

46115 *Scots Guardsman* was tested on 11 July 2008, after a thirty-year hiatus since its previous appearance on the main line, and is noted climbing through Langho en route to Blackburn still in grey primer.

The Stanier 3-cylinder locomotives were prone to problems and 46115 *Scots Guardsman* proved to be no exception in the early days of its return to main line service. After each occasion when repairs were made, a further loaded test run was undertaken to confirm the efficacy of the repairs.

46115 *Scots Guardsman* climbs through Longpreston on 27 April 2010 whilst approaching Hellifield with its post-repair loaded test run …

… and was later noted passing Brock as it headed north to Carnforth.

46115 *Scots Guardsman* departs from Hellifield at dusk on 5 February 2009 with a loaded test run after completion of repairs.

Opposite page

Bearing the temporary identity of 46168 *Girl Guide*, 46115 *Scots Guardsman* begins the climb out of Liverpool Lime St on 6 September 2009 with a charter to York on behalf of local Girl Guides.

This page

Right: Making its first revenue run after a successful loaded test run on 11 July 2008, 46115 *Scots Guardsman* races past Euxton Junction on 6 September 2008 with a Carnforth–Chester charter routed via Hellifield and Blackburn.

Below Left: 46115 *Scots Guardsman* races south through Brock on 9 May 2009 with the Carlisle–Preston leg of a railtour returning from Carlisle to Birmingham New St.

Below Right: 46115 *Scots Guardsman* races through Salwick on 9 August 2009 whilst working a one-way Carnforth–Blackpool North charter.

Left: 46115 *Scots Guardsman* curves through the Lune Gorge at Borrow Beck on 21 March 2015 whilst working the Carnforth–Carlisle leg of a Euston–Carlisle railtour whilst ...

Above: ... 46115 *Scots Guardsman* curves through Greenholme during its ascent of Shap on 9 April 2009 whilst working the Preston–Glasgow Central leg of the GREAT BRITAIN II railtour.

46115 *Scots Guardsman* storms out of Hellifield on 29 November 2008 after a water stop whilst working a Carnforth–Scarborough charter.

Left: 46115 *Scots Guardsman* follows the Kent Estuary at Meathop on 19 June 2010 whilst working the Carnforth–Ravenglass leg of a railtour from Birmingham

Below: and crosses the estuary at Arnside on its return to Carnforth where it will be replaced by a diesel locomotive for the Carnforth–Birmingham leg of the journey.

46115 *Scots Guardsman* curves through Helwith Bridge on 7 February 2009 whilst working the Hellifield–Carlisle leg of a Manchester Victoria–Carlisle railtour.

46115 *Scots Guardsman* climbs out of Settle on 2 August 2009 whilst working the seasonal WAVERLEY EXPRESS from York to Carlisle.

Left: 46115 *Scots Guardsman* breasts Ais Gill summit on 25 June 2011 whilst powering the Carlisle–Hellifield leg of a railtour from Carlisle returning to Leicester.

Below Left: 46115 *Scots Guardsman* climbs out of the Ribble Valley on 26 June 2013 as it passes Langho with the seasonal FELLSMAN service returning from Carlisle to Lancaster via the S&C route, Hellifield and Blackburn.

Below Right: 46115 *Scots Guardsman* crosses Whalley Viaduct over the River Calder on 4 September 2009 whilst working a Carnforth–Chester charter via Hellifield and Blackburn.

46115 *Scots Guardsman* drifts off Ribblehead Viaduct on 16 August 2008 whilst working the seasonal THAMES-CLYDE EXPRESS returning from Carlisle to York.

46115 *Scots Guardsman* bursts out of Blea Moor Tunnel on 1 June 2011 with the Hellifield–Carlisle leg of a Worcester–Carlisle railtour.

46115 *Scots Guardsman* curves onto the Burnley line at Hall Royd Junction on 17 July 2010 whilst working the COTTON MILL EXPRESS circular railtour from Manchester Victoria.

46115 *Scots Guardsman* curves through Oubeck on 9 February 2009 whilst working the Preston–Carlisle leg of a Birmingham New St–Carlisle railtour.

46115 *Scots Guardsman* climbs through Selside on 11 August 2010 with the seasonal FELLSMAN (Lancaster–Carlisle) service via Preston, Hellifield and the S&C route.

STANIER 'PRINCESS ROYAL' CLASS 4-6-2
BR = 46200–46212

This class was introduced by Sir William Stanier in 1933 when two locomotives, 6200 and 6201, were built at Crewe Works to haul the heaviest WCML trains, plus a third locomotive, 6202, to test a turbine arrangement. In essence the first pair are considered by many to be the 'Pacific' version of the GWR's 'Castle' class, given Stanier's previous employment at Swindon.

The first pair was subsequently followed in 1935 by an order for ten locomotives, 6203–6212, with design modifications learned from the operations of the first duo.

The class members worked services until 1962 when they were replaced by first diesel traction, then electric traction, but two locomotives survived into preservation. These were (4)6201 *Princess Elizabeth*, named after the present Queen, and (4)6203 *Princess Margaret Rose*, named after her sister.

Throughout preservation (4)6201 *Princess Elizabeth* has been maintained in LMSR Lined Maroon livery and fleet number whilst, as at December 2016, 46203 *Princess Margaret Rose* is undergoing overhaul at the Midland Railway Centre (Butterley).

Right: 6201 *Princess Elizabeth* awaits departure from Liverpool Lime St on 1 April 2006 with a railtour returning to Euston.

Far Right: 46203 *Princess Margaret Rose* climbs out of the Ribble Valley as it passes Billington on 29 August 1994 with the Carlisle–Crewe leg of a railtour returning from Carlisle to Euston.

6201 *Princess Elizabeth* curves through Greenholme on 3 April 2004 whilst ascending Shap with the Crewe–Carlisle leg of a Bristol–Carlisle railtour.

46203 *Princess Margaret Rose* begins the climb out of the Ribble Valley at Billington on 6 July 1991 whilst working the Carlisle–Crewe leg of a railtour returning from Carlisle to Euston.

6201 *Princess Elizabeth* climbs out of the Ribble Valley at Langho on 30 June 2007 whilst working the Carlisle–Crewe leg of a railtour returning from Carlisle to Gloucester.

6201 *Princess Elizabeth* accelerates off the Ribblehead Viaduct on 10 June 2006 whilst working the Hellifield–Carlisle leg of a Bedford–Carlisle railtour.

Left: 6201 *Princess Elizabeth* awaits the 'right-away' at Preston on 7 September 2002 after a water stop whilst working a railtour returning from Carlisle to Liverpool Lime St.

Below: 6201 *Princess Elizabeth* speeds away from Preston on 11 May 2002, with its support coach, after completing the Carlisle–Preston leg of a southbound railtour and returning to its then base at Bury on the East Lancashire Railway.

6201 *Princess Elizabeth* curves over Lunds Viaduct on 7 February 1987 whilst working a Euston–Carlisle railtour.

Opposite page

Left: 6201 *Princess Elizabeth* accelerates through Lostock Hall on 28 July 2007 whilst working the Preston–Carlisle leg of a Manchester Victoria–Carlisle railtour.

Top: 6201 *Princess Elizabeth* pauses at Garsdale for a water stop on 20 July 1991 whilst working a CUMBRIAN MOUNTAIN EXPRESS railtour from Euston to Carlisle.

Below: 6201 *Princess Elizabeth* joins the WCML at Golborne Junction on 7 September 2002 whilst working a MERSEYSIDE EXPRESS railtour from Liverpool Lime St to Carlisle.

This page

Left: 6201 *Princess Elizabeth* curves through Oubeck on 16 November 2006 whilst working the Preston–Glasgow Central leg of a Euston–Glasgow Central railtour.

Below Left: 6201 *Princess Elizabeth* speeds through Balshaw Lane Junction on 12 November 2011 whilst working a Birmingham–Carlisle railtour.

Below Right: 6201 *Princess Elizabeth* curves over Lunds Viaduct on 1 June 2002 with a Preston–Carlisle railtour.

Right: 6201 *Princess Elizabeth* drifts through Clitheroe, under the shadow of Clitheroe Castle, on 29 August 2005 whilst working a railtour returning from Carlisle to Euston.

Below Left: 6201 *Princess Elizabeth* climbs through Langho on 7 August 2010 whilst returning with a CUMBRIAN MOUNTAIN EXPRESS railtour from Carlisle to Liverpool Lime St.

Below Right: 6201 *Princess Elizabeth* drifts past Bamber Bridge signal box on 26 April 2003 whilst working the Carlisle–Crewe leg of a railtour returning from Carlisle to Slough.

6201 *Princess Elizabeth* enters the tunnel at Liverpool Lime St at the start of its climb to Edge Hill on 7 August 2010 whilst working a railtour to Carlisle.

6201 *Princess Elizabeth* stands in Liverpool
Lime St on 6 June 2003 after its arrival with a
MERSEYSIDE EXPRESS railtour returning from
Euston.

Left: 6201 *Princess Elizabeth* climbs away from Settle Junction at the start of the 'Long Drag' to Ais Gill on 9 June 2007 whilst working the Preston–Carlisle leg of a Bedford–Carlisle railtour.

Below Left: 6201 *Princess Elizabeth* drifts through Docker on 1 June 2002 whilst working a railtour returning from Carlisle to Preston.

Below Right: 6201 *Princess Elizabeth* races past Hale as it nears Liverpool on 10 February 2007 whilst working a Euston–Liverpool Lime St railtour.

STANIER 'CORONATION' CLASS 4-6-2
BR = 46220–46257

This class was introduced by Sir William Stanier in 1937, both as a development of his 'Princess Royal' class and as a response to the success of Gresley's 'A4' class design. To meet the latter need, the early locomotives (6220–6229; 6235–6248) were originally streamlined although this was removed from 1946. The final pair (6256 and 6257) were authorised by H.G. Ivatt in 1947 and built with the latest developments to provide comparison with the pair of his Derby-built diesel locomotives (10000–1); a single locomotive to be the equivalent of a Stanier Class 5 4-6-0 and the pair to be the equivalent of a single 'Coronation' class locomotive.

The fleet was rapidly withdrawn between 1962 and 1964 with two locomotives being sold to Billy Butlin's Holiday Camps as display items: 46229 *Duchess of Hamilton* sited at Minehead and 46233 *Duchess of Sutherland* sited at Ayr. These were later recovered for preservation with 46229 joining the National Rail Museum's fleet at York and 46233 being bought privately and based at the Midland Railway Centre (Butterley). Both locomotives have operated on the main line in various guises and liveries bearing either their LMSR or BR fleet numbers.

46229 *Duchess of Hamilton* **accelerates through Ribblehead on 28 July 1990 whilst working the southbound CUMBRIAN MOUNTAIN EXPRESS returning from Carlisle to Euston.**

46229 *Duchess of Hamilton* spent a brief sojourn on the East Lancashire Railway during 1995/96 and returned to its York base on 30 March 1996 by powering a Preston–Scarborough railtour that called at Wigan North Western to collect passengers.

Above: 46229 *Duchess of Hamilton* curves into the approach to Wigan and …

Right: … awaits the 'right-away' to continue its journey.

BY ROYAL APPOINTMENT

On 11 May 2002 46233 *Duchess of Sutherland*, bearing LMSR Lined Maroon livery and fleet number, was selected to power the Royal Train during a tour of North Wales undertaken by H.R.H. The Queen, to become the first steam locomotive on Royal duty since 1968.

To mark the success of the occasion, the locomotive was granted the right to bear the Royal Crest above its nameplate as noted on the second Royal Train on 22 March 2005 when H.M. Prince Charles, a known rail supporter, toured the Settle & Carlisle communities by rail.

The Royal Train stands at Bangor after its arrival with the Royal party and awaits the next stage of its tour programme.

46233 *Duchess of Sutherland* breasts Ais Gill Summit whilst heading north en route to a Kirkby Stephen call with H.M. Prince Charles reportedly on the footplate.

46233 *Duchess of Sutherland*, bearing LMSR Lined Maroon livery and fleet number, drifts into Hellifield on 5 August 2006 in preparation for a locomotive exchange whilst working the Carlisle–Hellifield leg of a railtour returning from Carlisle to Kettering.

46233 *Duchess of Sutherland*, bearing BR Lined Green livery and fleet number, storms through the Lune Gorge at Borrow Beck on 7 February 2015 whilst powering the Carnforth–Carlisle leg of a Euston–Carlisle railtour.

46233 *Duchess of Sutherland*, bearing LMSR Lined Maroon livery and fleet number, curves through Beckfoot on 14 June 2003 whilst working the Crewe–Carlisle leg of a Northampton–Carlisle railtour.

46233 *Duchess of Sutherland*, bearing LMSR Lined Maroon livery and fleet number, approaches Leyland on 19 April 2003 whilst working a charter returning from Blackpool North to Chesterfield.

46233 *Duchess of Sutherland* bearing BR Lined Green livery and fleet number, curves through Greenholme on 31 January 2015 whilst powering the Carnforth–Carlisle leg of a Euston–Carlisle railtour on its ascent of Shap.

Following a major overhaul, the members of the owning group of 6233/46233 *Duchess of Sutherland* voted to operate the locomotive in other guises that it had carried during its service with both the LMSR and BR companies. By coincidence the three guises were photographed at the same location – Euxton – as shown on this page:

Left: Bearing LMSR Lined Maroon livery and fleet number on 3 June 2006 whilst powering a railtour returning from Carlisle to Crewe.

Below Left: Bearing LMSR Lined Black livery and fleet number on 8 May 2010 whilst powering the Carlisle–Crewe leg of a railtour returning from Carlisle to Gloucester.

Below Right: Bearing BR Lined Green livery and fleet number on 9 June 2012 whilst powering the Carlisle–Crewe leg of a railtour returning from Carlisle to Milton Keynes.

46233 *Duchess of Sutherland* curves through Greenholme on 14 June 2012 as it ascends Shap whilst working the Carnforth–Carlisle leg of a Euston–Carlisle railtour.

46233 *Duchess of Sutherland*, bearing LMSR Lined Maroon livery and fleet number, climbs to Copy Pit on 29 June 2003 whilst working the outward leg of a Chester–Leeds VSOE charter.

Left: 46233 *Duchess of Sutherland*, bearing LMSR Lined Maroon livery and fleet number, breasts Hoghton Summit on 28 April 2005 whilst working the outward leg of a Lincoln–Carlisle VSOE charter.

Below: 46233 *Duchess of Sutherland*, bearing LMSR Lined Black livery and fleet number, is 'panned' on 21 August 2010 as it nears Ais Gill summit whilst working a railtour returning from Carlisle to Liverpool Lime St.

Right: 46233 *Duchess of Sutherland*, bearing LMSR Lined Black livery and fleet number, races through Brock on 8 August 2010 whilst working the Crewe–Carlisle leg of a Gloucester–Carlisle railtour.

Below Left: 46233 *Duchess of Sutherland*, bearing LMSR Lined Maroon livery and fleet number, climbs up to Leyland on 13 April 2002 with a charter returning from Blackpool North to Sheffield.

Below Right: 46233 *Duchess of Sutherland*, bearing LMSR Lined Maroon livery and fleet number, curves past Armathwaite on 7 July 2007 with a railtour returning from Carlisle to Liverpool Lime St.

Left: 46233 *Duchess of Sutherland*, bearing LMSR Lined Maroon livery and fleet number, races out of Culgaith Tunnel on 3 July 2004 whilst working a railtour returning from Carlisle to Leicester.

Bottom Left: 46233 *Duchess of Sutherland*, bearing LMSR Lined Maroon livery and fleet number, approaches the closed Rimington station on 2 July 2005 whilst working the Crewe–Carlisle leg of a Bristol–Carlisle railtour.

Below Right: 46233 *Duchess of Sutherland*, bearing LMSR Lined Maroon livery and fleet number, accelerates past Bamber Bridge on 19 June 2004 whilst working the outward leg of a Northampton–Carlisle railtour.

46233 *Duchess of Sutherland*, bearing BR Lined Green livery and fleet number, curves off Ribblehead Viaduct on 7 February 2015 whilst working the Carlisle–Farington Junction leg of a railtour returning from Carlisle to Euston.

46233 *Duchess of Sutherland*, bearing BR Lined Green livery and fleet number, climbs away from Settle on 2 June 2012 as it starts the ascent of the 'Long Drag' to Ais Gill whilst working a Lincoln–Leeds–Carlisle–Tyne Valley–Newcastle–Doncaster–Lincoln railtour.

IVATT CLASS 2MT 2-6-0
BR = 46400–46527

This class was designed by H.G. Ivatt to both replace the mix of 0-6-0 designs inherited by the LMSR at the 1923 Grouping and replenish the LMSR's locomotive fleet following the end of the Second World War. The design was a variant of his Class 2MT 2-6-2T design (BR = 41200–41321) and proved sufficiently successful that R.A. Riddles adopted it, with minimum changes, as his Standard Class 2 locomotive design (fleet number 78000–78064) whilst Ivatt's 2-6-2T design was adopted by Riddles as his Standard Class 2 Tank locomotive design (BR = 84000–84029).

The seven preserved examples of this class are normally to be found on heritage lines hence appearances on the main line are extremely rare; this includes 46441 that

was bought by the Beet family when it was withdrawn from BR service at Carnforth in April 1967. In 1995 the Beet family was offered an opportunity to use 46441 on a special Dining Train charter that ran from Liverpool Lime St via Wigan Wallgate to Southport where the train was shunted to return to Liverpool via the electric network to Bootle thence via the Bootle branch to Edge Hill and Liverpool Lime St. As at December 2016, this locomotive is on display at the Ribble Steam Railway Museum in Preston where it is on long-term loan from the Beet family.

46441, bearing LMSR Lined Maroon livery with BR fleet number and THE MERSEYSIDE EXPRESS headboard, curves into Southport on 19 March 1995 with the Liverpool Dining Train at the end of the first stage of its Merseyside tour.

FOWLER 3F 0-6-0T
BR = 47260–47681

This design was introduced by Sir Henry Fowler in 1924 as a development of an earlier Midland Railway design with detail differences. The class was distributed throughout the LMSR and proved to be a popular and reliable design, able to work a variety of services from yard shunting to local passenger with equal competency. Ten examples of this class survive, despite the fact that class members were quickly replaced by the standard Class 08 diesel shunting locomotive hence scrapped before thoughts of preservation existed, let alone acted on.

No class members have main line certification as at December 2016 but, in September 1982, Southport was host to a joint exhibition of rolling stock from both BR and the adjacent Steamport Museum, at the end of which BR had arranged for a class 03 to transfer Steamport stock to its boundary with BR. A Steamport locomotive was provided to collect the consist from the boundary but, when the Class 03 shunter failed with gearbox problems, the Steamport locomotive was authorised to operate on BR lines to collect the Steamport stock from Southport station and return it to Steamport.

47298 was rescued from Barry Scrapyard in July 1974 and restored to working order at Southport (Steamport). Restored in LMSR Unlined Black livery with LMSR fleet number, 47298 draws away from Southport station on 12 September 1982 after collecting the rolling stock for transfer to Steamport Museum.

STANIER CLASS 8F 2-8-0
BR = 48000–48775

This class was designed by Sir William Stanier as a standard freight locomotive to replace the plethora of heavy freight designs inherited by the LMSR at the 1923 Grouping. The first batch was built by Crewe Works but subsequent orders were also placed with outside builders such as Vulcan Foundry and the North British Locomotive Company. In 1938 the Ministry of Supply (MOS) adopted the design for wartime use hence further orders were placed at the MOS's behest with both private companies and the workshops of the other three post-Grouping railway companies.

A total of 849 locomotives were built but many were sent immediately overseas after delivery; some were lost when the ships carrying them were sunk through enemy action. At the end of the Second World War, some class members were retained for use by liberated countries, some were retained by the War Department and some were retained by other post-Grouping railway companies to supplement their war-ravaged locomotive fleets but, by 1946, the post-Grouping companies had relinquished ownership to the LMSR.

The LMSR finally ended up with 665 locomotives, some of which continued to operate until the end of steam traction in August 1968. Although nominally a freight locomotive, some class members had their wheels balanced to allow their use on fast freight services which, consequently, also saw their use hauling occasional passenger services and excursion trains.

As at December 2016 there are six class members preserved, plus two examples repatriated from abroad, but only 48151, rescued from Barry Scrapyard in November 1975, is certified for main line running. It is based at the Carnforth site of the West Coast Railway Company (WCRC), from where it often hauls railtours and charter services in the North of England.

At the end of the twentieth century 48773, based on the Severn Valley Railway, was certified for main line operation and, on 24 April 1999, it was paired with Stanier Class 5 4-6-0 45407 as they ascended Daisyfield Bank past Daisyfield whilst working the Farington Junction–Carlisle leg of the CUMBRIAN MOUNTAIN EXPRESS railtour from Euston to Carlisle.

48151 *Gauge O Guild* coasts off Ribblehead Viaduct on 18 August 2010 whilst working the seasonal FELLSMAN service returning from Carlisle to Lancaster.

48151 crosses the Kent Estuary as it approaches Arnside on 16 July 2005 whilst working a railtour returning from Sellafield to Carnforth.

Left: 48151 stands in Southport on 4 April 2012 after returning from its day's outing to York.

Below: Making a rare (steam) locomotive visit to Southport, 48151 awaits departure on 4 April 2012 with a charter to York as a local service train arrives from Manchester.

48151 *Gauge O Guild* curves past Armathwaite on 4 August 2010 with THE FELLSMAN seasonal railtour returning from Carlisle to Lancaster.

48151 *Gauge O Guild* climbs away from Settle on 25 July 2010 with THE WAVERLEY seasonal railtour from York to Carlisle.

48151 *Gauge O Guild* crosses Arten Gill viaduct on 26 August 2007 whilst working a Hellifield–Carlisle railtour.

48151 *Gauge O Guild* crosses the River Weaver at Frodsham on 11 March 2006 whilst working a Carnforth–Chester charter.

Dawn breaks over the northern fells on 13 March 2007 as 48151 *Gauge O Guild* curves through Scout Green whilst powering a stock move from Carnforth (WCRC) to Inverness.

48151 curves through Oubeck on 23 July 2014 shortly after leaving Lancaster with THE FELLSMAN seasonal service from Lancaster to Carlisle via the Settle & Carlisle route.

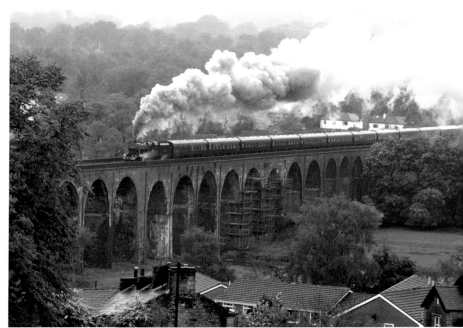

Left: 48151 *Gauge O Guild* pilots Standard Class 7 'Britannia' 4-6-2 70013 *Oliver Cromwell*, bearing the temporary guise of 70048 *The Territorial Army* 1908–2008, as they curve through Mossley on 27 March 2010 with a Lancaster–York charter run in support of the 'Help For Heroes' charity.

Above: 48151 *Gauge O Guild* crosses Whalley Viaduct on 20 May 2006 whilst working the Hellifield–Lancaster leg of a Skegness–Lancaster charter.

Below: Following a major overhaul 48151 was required to undergo a loaded test run on the Carnforth Circuit before regaining its main line certification. The test train is noted passing Longpreston on 18 March 2010 as it approached Hellifield where a water stop was taken and checks made of the locomotive.

FOWLER S&DJR 7F 2-8-0
BR = 53800–53810

This class was introduced by Sir Henry Fowler in 1914 to power services on the Somerset & Dorset Joint Railway (S&DJR), running between Bath and Bournemouth, for which the Midland Railway provided motive power. A second batch (53806–53810) was built by the LMSR in 1925 but with a larger boiler and detail alterations, although these were subsequently rebuilt to the original small boiler design by BR.

Two locomotives entered preservation after rescue from Barry Scrapyard; as at December 2016 53808, rescued in October 1970, is based on the West Somerset Railway (WSR) whilst 53809, rescued in 1975, moved to the Midland Railway Centre (Butterley) in March 1980 but is on loan to the WSR. Neither locomotive has current main line certification.

53809, bearing LMSR Unlined Black livery and fleet number, powers up Giggleswick Bank on 14 April 1984 whilst working the Hellifield–Carnforth leg of the CUMBRIAN MOUNTAIN EXPRESS railtour returning from Carlisle to Euston.

WEBB LNWR COAL TANK 0-6-2T
BR = 58880–58937

This class was introduced by F.W. Webb in 1881 as a tank version of his standard 17-inch tender locomotive, known as 'Coal Engines' because of their allocation to slow freight trains. Three hundred locomotives were built between 1881 and 1897 with 292 examples passing to the LMSR at the 1923 Grouping and 64 passing to BR at the 1948 Nationalisation. Not all examples survived long enough to carry BR fleet numbers but 58926, now preserved but restricted to use on heritage lines as at December 2016, carries its previous LNWR (1054), LMSR (7799) and BR (58926) fleet numbers at various times.

58926 entered preservation after withdrawal from BR service in 1958 and, as at December 2016, is based on the Keighley & Worth Valley Railway but on long-term loan to the Foxfield Steam Railway.

Wilson's Brewery, based in the Manchester suburb of Miles Patting, celebrated its 150th Anniversary in 1984 and, during July and August 1984, celebrated the event by chartering a number of trains to run between Manchester Victoria and its private siding at Miles Platting where special platforms were built to allow passengers to detrain.

The train comprised 58926, making a rare appearance on the main line, and the preserved Caledonian Railway coach but the service was restricted to trade personnel hence was not available to the general public.

Above: 58926 stands at the platform in Manchester Victoria on 11 July 1984 awaiting departure to the brewery.

Below: 58926 runs through the centre road at Manchester Victoria on 11 July 1984 en route to Newton Heath depot for maintenance and re-coaling.

Section 2:
Western Region (WR)

On 1 January 1923 the Transport Act 1922 became effective and grouped the railway network of the day into four separate companies with companies in the West of England and South Wales becoming part of the Great Western Railway Company (GWR). This grouping of railway companies changed little as most of the minor railways had either already been absorbed by the pre-Grouping company or were operated by it.

On 1 January 1948, when the railways were nationalised under the Transport Act 1947, the four Grouping companies became regions of the new British Railways (BR) with the GWR then becoming British Railways Western Region (BR(WR)) and its locomotive fleet retaining its fleet numbers without change. Its class sequencing was not quite in numerical order however, but sequenced by the second digit of the 4-digit fleet number.

COLLETT 'CASTLE' CLASS 4-6-0
BR = 4037; 4074–4099; 5000–5099; 7000–7037

This class was introduced by Charles Collett in 1923 as a development of the GWR 'Star' Class 4-6-0 and construction carried through until BR days when the final locomotive, 7037 *Swindon,* was released from Swindon Works in August 1950. The class was allocated to the major expresses throughout the WR and, as at December 2016, eight locomotives have been preserved although not all are available for main line operation.

Left: 5043 *Earl of Mount Edgcumbe* curves through Mossley on 16 April 2011 whilst working a railtour from Tyseley to Blackburn via the Standedge and Calder Valley routes.

Right: 5029 *Nunney Castle* joins the West Coast Main Line at Balshaw Lane Junction on 24 February 2011 whilst working the Preston–Bristol leg of THE GREAT BRITAIN IV railtour, the fourth year of this annual tour of the UK behind as many steam locomotives that are available.

5043 *Earl of Mount Edgcumbe* powers off Ribblehead Viaduct on 10 March 2012 with a railtour returning from Carlisle to Tyseley. This train should have included Stanier 'Princess Royal' Class 4-6-2 6201 *Princess Elizabeth*, which had worked on the outward service but was failed at Carlisle prior to departure, hence 5043 being permitted to haul the returning train without assistance.

In 1994 5029 *Nunney Castle* was operated over the Settle & Carlisle route when it powered the Crewe–Carlisle leg of a Swindon–Carlisle railtour on 12 February 1994. Scenes from the day include:

Left: 5029 *Nunney Castle* nearing the summit of 'The Long Drag' from Settle at Ais Gill and

Below: leaving Appleby after a stop for water.

Right: 5043 *Earl of Mount Edgcumbe* curves through Greenholme on 20 June 2009 on its ascent of Shap whilst working the outward leg of a Birmingham New St–Carlisle railtour.

Below Left: 5043 *Earl of Mount Edgcumbe* pilots Stanier 'Coronation' Class 4-6-2 46233 *Duchess of Sutherland* through Greenholme on 15 June 2013 as they ascend Shap with the outward leg of a Tyseley–Carlisle railtour.

Below Right: 5043 *Earl of Mount Edgcumbe* nears Copy Pit summit on 16 April 2011 whilst working a railtour from Tyseley to Blackburn via the Standedge and Calder Valley routes.

COLLETT 'KING' CLASS 4-6-0
BR = 6000–6029

This class was introduced by Charles Collett in 1927 as a development of his earlier 'Castle' Class design; it introduced the most powerful 4-6-0 design within the UK but the power came with an axle-weight that restricted it to specified routes to Bristol, Cardiff, Plymouth and Wolverhampton. The introduction of the Class 52 diesel hydraulic fleet in 1963 resulted in the mass withdrawal of the fleet from which only three class members survived.

Class doyen 6000 *King George V* became part of the National Collection on withdrawal and was the guinea pig for the trials conducted in October 1971 that led to the easing of restrictions on steam operations on the BR network.

Class members 6023 *King Edward II* and 6024 *King Edward I* were both rescued from the Barry Scrapyard and restored to working order; as at December 2016 their main activity has been on heritage lines with minimum appearances on the national network.

Of educational interest is that the naming of the class reflects the Kings of England in reverse order from King George V who was reigning at the time of the introduction of the class.

6024 *King Edward I* curves through Daisyfield, on the outskirts of Blackburn, on 28 March 1998 whilst working a Swindon–Carlisle railtour routed via the Ribble Valley and the Settle & Carlisle routes.

COLLETT 'HALL' CLASS 4-6-0
BR = 4900–4999; 5900–5999; 6900–6958

This class was introduced by Charles Collett in 1928, as a development of G.J. Churchward's 'Saint' Class 4-6-0, intended for mixed traffic duties and on which Sir William Stanier based his Class 5 4-6-0 design that he introduced to the LMSR during the 1930s.

F.W. Hawksworth introduced an improved design from 1944 but these are identified as a separate class rather than a modification within an existing class.

As at December 2016 ten class members have been preserved with only the Tyseley-based locomotives certified for main line service. Of note is that 5972 *Olton Hall*, owned by David Smith, was contracted to the role of *Hogwarts Castle* for the *Harry Potter* films.

Right: 4936 *Kinlet Hall* climbs up to Leyland on 17 July 2004 with a charter returning from Blackpool North to Tyseley.

Below: 4965 *Rood Ashton Hall* pilots 4936 *Kinlet Hall* as they curve through Oubeck on 18 May 2002 with a railtour from Tyseley to Carlisle via the main WCML route over Shap.

5972 *Olton Hall* **curves through Helwith Bridge on 19 December 1999 with a charter from Hellifield to Carlisle.**

5972 *Olton Hall* has gained fame from its adaption to *Hogwarts Castle* to star in the *Harry Potter* series of films. The contract with Warner brothers, the film-makers, includes severe restrictions on the locomotive's usage and the carrying of its *Hogwarts Castle* nameplates which are eased when the locomotive carries its *Olton Hall* nameplates. 5972 made its last runs as *Hogwarts Castle* in July 2014 after which it was moved to the Warner Brothers film studios in Watford to become a static display item in the Harry Potter Exhibition for an initial two-year period.

Right: 5972 bears its original *Olton Hall* nameplates on 28 April 2001 as it passes Balshaw Lane Junction with a charter from Carnforth to Holyhead.

Below: 5972 is 'in character' as *Hogwarts Castle* on 7 June 2014 whilst working the Carnforth–York leg of THE WIZARD EXPRESS from Manchester Victoria to York via Carnforth.

Section 3:
Southern Region (SR)

On 1 January 1923 the Transport Act 1922 became effective and grouped the railway network of the day into four separate companies with companies south of the Thames, on the south coast extending to Weymouth and the routes of the London South Western Railway (LSWR) extending into Devon and Cornwall becoming part of the Southern Railway Company (SR).

On 1 January 1948, when the railways were nationalised under the Transport Act 1947, the four Grouping companies became regions of the new British Railways (BR) with the SR then becoming British Railways Southern Region (BR(SR)) and its locomotive fleet adding 30000 to its fleet numbers. The mix of locomotives had never fully been rationalised during the post-Grouping era; fleet numbers had been allocated to fill gaps during pre-Grouping days and only new locomotives during post-Grouping days had been allocated blocks of fleet numbers and this remained unaltered in the post-Nationalisation days.

URIE N15 'KING ARTHUR' CLASS 4-6-0
BR = 30448–30457; 30736–30755; 30763–30806

This class was initially introduced by R.W. Urie in 1919 to haul the LSWR's heaviest expresses. After the 1923 Grouping, the SR's Publicity Department named the locomotives after Arthurian characters (hence the class becoming identified as 'King Arthur') whilst R.E.L. Maunsell improved the design and ordered further locomotives from both Eastleigh Works and the North British Locomotive Company (NBL).

30777 *Sir Lamiel* entered preservation as part of the National Collection when withdrawn from service in October 1961 and, as at December 2016, is now part of the NRM's fleet albeit based at the Great Central Railway under the care of the 5305 Locomotive Association.

The class was subjected to tests with smoke deflectors by R.E.L. Maunsell and, in preservation, 777/30777 has adopted both guises at various times.

Above: 30777 *Sir Lamiel*, bearing SR livery, fleet number and without smoke deflectors, nears the summit at Ais Gill on 26 May 1990 with the Carlisle–Hellifield leg of a railtour returning from Carlisle to Euston.

Below: 30777 *Sir Lamiel*, bearing BR livery, fleet number and with smoke deflectors, curves off Ribblehead Viaduct on 6 August 2006 whilst working a railtour returning from Carlisle to York.

URIE S15 CLASS 4-6-0
BR = 30496–30515; 30823–30837; 30838–30847

This class was initially introduced by R.W. Urie in 1920 for mixed traffic duties on the LSWR. After the 1923 Grouping Maunsell improved the design and ordered a second batch of fifteen locomotives from Eastleigh Works followed by further design improvements and an order for ten locomotives in 1936.

As at December 2016 four class members are preserved but none has main line certification.

30828, bearing SR Malachite Green livery and fleet number, makes a water stop at Appleby on 7 May 1994 whilst working the Carlisle–Hellifield leg of a railtour returning from Carlisle to Kings Cross.

MAUNSELL 'LORD NELSON' CLASS 4-6-0
BR = 30850–30864

This class was introduced by R.E.L. Maunsell in 1925 to haul the heaviest expresses, including the Southampton Boat Trains, on the South Western Division of the SR. Initially found to be 'troublesome' the class underwent many experiments to identify – and solve – their unpredictable performances.

30850 *Lord Nelson* is the only surviving class member and joined the National Collection when withdrawn from BR service in August 1962. As at December 2016, it is part of the NRM collection but is based on the Mid-Hants Railway with overhauls contracted to Eastleigh Works where engineering skills are still available.

Right: 30850 *Lord Nelson*, bearing SR Malachite Green livery and fleet number, is wreathed in steam at Manchester Victoria on the evening of 8 October 1983 as it makes a water stop whilst en route from Carnforth to York.

Below: 30850 *Lord Nelson*, in SR Malachite Green livery and fleet number, approaches Culgaith Tunnel on 24 August 1985 whilst working the Hellifield–Carlisle leg of the CUMBRIAN MOUNTAIN PULLMAN railtour from Kings Cross to Carlisle.

BULLEID 'WEST COUNTRY' CLASS 4-6-0
BR = 34001 4048; 34091–34108

BULLEID 'BATTLE OF BRITAIN' CLASS 4-6-0
BR = 34049–34090; 34109–34110

This class was introduced by O.V. Bulleid in 1945 as a lighter version of his 'Merchant Navy' Class design and intended as a standard mixed traffic design to replace the multitude of mixed traffic and tank locomotive designs then operating on the SR network. Once the 'Merchant Navy' class had been rebuilt into more conventional form, attention turned to this class and batches of conversions were authorised. The implementation of the 1954 Modernisation Plan brought this programme to an end, resulting in both original and rebuilt locomotives working until the end of steam on the SR in July 1967.

As at December 2016 there are eight (including three unrebuilt) West Country class members and twelve (including eight unrebuilt) Battle of Britain class members preserved with two (34046 *Braunton* (temporarily running as 34052 *Lord Dowding*) and 34067 *Tangmere*) having main line certification.

34067 *Tangmere* is normally based in the London area but returns north to the West Coast Railway Company (WCRC) base at Carnforth for overhaul and repairs, after which it undergoes a main line loaded test run on the Carnforth Circuit via Hellifield, Blackburn and Preston. On 8 February 2011, 34067 *Tangmere* curves away from Hellifield with its test train en route to Blackburn following completion of its latest overhaul.

34067 *Tangmere* climbs through Longpreston on 8 February 2011 whilst approaching Hellifield with its loaded test run on the Carnforth Circuit after completion of its latest overhaul.

Left: 34067 *Tangmere* was originally restored to main line condition by Ian Riley at his engineering works, located on the East Lancashire Railway, following which the locomotive was sent to Crewe for weighing before undertaking a loaded test run. 34067 *Tangmere* was noted passing Winwick on 24 February 2003 en route to Crewe for weighing.

Below: Once a successful test cycle was completed, the first main line run for 34067 *Tangmere* was on 1 March 2003 when it worked the Preston–Carlisle leg of a Bristol–Carlisle railtour. 34067 *Tangmere* is seen curving through Oubeck en route to Carlisle but, sadly, the locomotive failed at Oxenholme and the engine was replaced by a pair of Class 57/3 locomotives travelling behind the railtour en route to Carlisle to take up their 'Thunderbird' duties for Virgin Trains.

Top Left 34067 *Tangmere* eases a Northampton–Morecambe railtour into Bare Lane whilst working in top 'n tail mode with Standard Class 4 2-6-0 76079 on this leg traversing the Lancaster to Morecambe branch.

Top Right: 34067 *Tangmere* restarts from a signal check at Euxton on 26 November 2014 whilst en route from Carnforth (WCRC) to Bristol Barton Hill to work a railtour in the West Country.

Below Right: 34092 *City of Wales* is based on the Keighley & Worth Valley Railway, from where it used to make main line appearances, as on 2 May 1983 when, in dreich Settle & Carlisle weather, it approached Ais Gill summit with the Carlisle–Hellifield leg of the southbound CUMBRIAN MOUNTAIN EXPRESS returning from Carlisle to Kings Cross.

Opposite page

34092 *City of Wells* climbs to Longpreston on 6 August 1988 with the Carlisle to Hellifield leg of the southbound CUMBRIAN MOUNTAIN EXPRESS returning from Carlisle to Euston. This was the locomotive's last main line appearance before withdrawal for major overhaul at its Haworth base on the Keighley & Worth Valley Railway. When the overhaul was completed during 2016, doubts were cast on the locomotive's return to the main line, given the cost of fitting the necessary equipment required for main line operation.

Right: 34027 *Taw Valley*, rebuilt to conventional form, drifts towards Farington Junction, where it will diverge to traverse the Ribble Valley and Settle & Carlisle routes, on 4 March 2000 whilst working the Crewe–Carlisle leg of a Euston–Carlisle railtour.

Below Left: 34046 *Braunton*, rebuilt to conventional form, crosses Whalley Viaduct above the Ribble Valley on 16 July 2013 whilst undertaking its loaded test run on the Carnforth Circuit prior to gaining its main line certification.

Below Right: 34046 *Braunton*, rebuilt to conventional form, curves out of Hellifield on 16 July 2013 whilst undertaking its loaded test run on the Carnforth Circuit prior to gaining its main line certification.

BULLEID 'MERCHANT NAVY' CLASS 4-6-2
BR = 35001–35030

This class was introduced in 1941 by O.V. Bulleid and incorporated many unconventional design features, including a chain-driven valve gear and air-smoothed body casing, which proved troublesome in service. During the 1950s the class was rebuilt to conventional form and served its operators until the cessation of steam on the SR in July 1967.

As at December 2016, ten class members have been preserved with only 35028 *Clan Line* having main line certification; in addition 35029 *Ellerman Lines* has been sectioned for display in the York site of the National Rail Museum.

Right: When first released to main line action, 35005 *Canadian Pacific* was in BR Blue livery, as trialled in the early days of Nationalisation, when it was noted passing Salwick on 16 October 1999 with the outward leg of a Nuneaton–Blackpool North charter.

Below Left: 35005 *Canadian Pacific* returned later in the day and was noted passing Salwick with the charter returning from Blackpool North to Nuneaton.

Below Right: 35028 *Clan Line* approaches the summit at Ais Gill on 8 April 1989 whilst working the Carlisle–Hellifield leg of a southbound CUMBRIAN MOUNTAIN EXPRESS returning from Carlisle to Kings Cross.

Section 4:
Eastern Region (ER)

On 1 January 1923 the Transport Act 1922 became effective and grouped the railway network of the day into four separate companies, with the four companies then operating the East Coast route between London and Aberdeen, and the companies operating to the east of it being merged to form the London North Eastern Railway (LNER).

On 1 January 1948, when the railways were nationalised under the Transport Act 1947, the four Grouping companies became regions of the new British Railways (BR) with the LNER then becoming British Railways Eastern Region (BR(ER))

and its locomotive fleet adding 60000 to its fleet numbers as a result. The mix of locomotives had never fully been rationalised during the post-Grouping era; fleet numbers had been allocated to fill gaps during pre-Grouping days and only new locomotives during post-Grouping days had been allocated blocks of fleet numbers. While two schemes had been started, since Edward Thompson took office, to allocate locomotive classes a specific block of numbers, this process was incomplete at Nationalisation hence the opportunity was taken to renumber the locomotive fleet into class blocks.

GRESLEY 'A4' CLASS 4-6-0
BR = 60001–60034

This class was introduced by Sir Nigel Gresley in 1935 as the prestige locomotive to haul the premier prestige expresses on the East Coast routes and the class of thirty-five locomotives was introduced in batches as new services were introduced. There was friendly rivalry between the LMSR and LNER locomotive fleets but, in 1938, the world speed record for steam locomotives was gained by 4468/60022 *Mallard* when it attained a confirmed speed of 126 mph. One locomotive was destroyed during a raid on York but thirty-four class members survived the Second World War to continue working until the 1960s.

Six locomotives entered preservation when withdrawn from service and, as at December 2016, two locomotives (60008 *Dwight D Eisenhower* and 60010 *Dominion of Canada*) are located abroad, one locomotive (60022 *Mallard*) is on permanent non-operational display in the York site of the NRM and three locomotives (60007 *Sir Nigel Gresley,* 60009 *Union of South Africa* and *60019 Bittern)* have main line certification.

The 50th Anniversary of the World Speed Record for Steam Traction being attained by 4468 *Mallard* was celebrated in 1988, with the locomotive being restored to working order and returned to main line service for a brief period. The short programme of charters was initiated in May 1988 when 60022, restored to original LNER condition as 4468 *Mallard,* worked a Marylebone–Scarborough Postal Charter commemorating the issue of a set of postage stamps celebrating the anniversary.

The 100th 4-6-2 (Pacific) locomotive built to a Gresley design was A4 4498 (BR = 60007) *Sir Nigel Gresley,* which the LNER directors elected to mark by naming the locomotive after its designer – a rare tribute to a designer currently alive. It was consequently bought for preservation when withdrawn from BR service in 1966.

4468 *Mallard* **curves through Miles Platting as it breasts the bank on 10 May 1988 whilst powering away from Manchester Victoria en route to Scarborough.**

4498 *Sir Nigel Gresley* **climbs through Horsforth on 30 April 1977 whilst en route from its long-standing base at NCB Philadelphia to a new base at Carnforth's Steamtown by working a York–Carnforth railtour.**

60007 *Sir Nigel Gresley*, bearing BR Lined Blue livery and fleet number, nears Hoghton Summit on 16 April 2008 whilst working its loaded test run on the Carnforth Circuit, following major overhaul, in order to gain its main line certification.

60007 *Sir Nigel Gresley*, bearing LNER Lined Garter Blue livery and fleet number, nears the summit at Ais Gill on 4 June 1988 with the Carlisle–Hellifield leg of the southbound CUMBRIAN MOUNTAIN EXPRESS railtour returning from Carlisle to Kings Cross.

60007 *Sir Nigel Gresley*, bearing BR Lined Blue livery and fleet number, powers away from Appleby on 1 November 2008 after its water stop whilst working the Hellifield–Carlisle leg of a railtour from Kings Cross to Carlisle; note the use of the corridor connection between the locomotive and its support coach.

60009 *Union of South Africa* curves through Greenholme on 2 February 2013 whilst ascending Shap with the Carnforth–Carlisle leg of a railtour from Euston to Carlisle.

ALL IN A DAY'S WORK

Above: 60009 *Union of South Africa* curves through Oubeck on 23 November 2002 whilst working the Crewe–Carlisle leg of a railtour from Birmingham New St to Carlisle. On the return leg, a locomotive exchange took place at Preston where …

Left: … the driver of 60009 awaited the signal to shunt to the siding where …

Below: … it had its tender filled with water before continuing its journey, with support coach, to its then base at Crewe Heritage Centre.

60019 *Bittern* ran for a period with two tenders, as seen on 27 March 2010 when it drifted through Chelford whilst working a Euston–Manchester Piccadilly railtour.

And on 20 May 2010 when it drifted off Ribblehead Viaduct whilst working the Carlisle–Hellifield leg of the southbound CATHEDRALS EXPRESS railtour returning from Carlisle to Kings Cross.

In preparation for the 75th anniversary, in 2013, of 4468 *Mallard* gaining the World Speed Record for Steam Locomotives, 60019 *Bittern* was restored to LNER guise with fleet number 4464, here seen catching the sunset at Ribblehead Viaduct on 24 May 2012 whilst working the Edinburgh–Longpreston leg of the CATHEDRALS EXPLORER charter.

60019 *Bittern*, in its LNER guise as 4464 is seen on 15 March 2014 passing Balshaw Lane Junction with the Crewe–Carlisle leg of a Tyseley–Carlisle railtour.

Gresley 'A3' CLASS 4-6-2
BR = 60035–60112

This class was introduced by Sir Nigel Gresley in 1922 to handle the increasingly heavy expresses on the East Coast route; initially designated Class 'A1', their later upgrade with higher pressure boilers led their re-designation as Class 'A3' when rebuilt or built from new to the later design. The most famous class member is 4472/60103 *Flying Scotsman* – principally because it was the first pacific locomotive released to the nascent LNER in 1923. It was bought privately for preservation when withdrawn from BR service in January 1963 and bought by the NRM in April 2004 when made available for sale by private tender.

Right: 4472 *Flying Scotsman* accelerates through Bamber Bridge on 19 October 2002 whilst working the outward leg of a Crewe–York NORTHERN BELLE charter.

Below: 4472 *Flying Scotsman* hustles up the WCML at Brock on 20 December 2005 on its last day of service before withdrawal for overhaul; expected to take a couple of years the locomotive finally regained the main line in January 2016 after protracted overhaul. Its final train was the transfer of stock from Tyseley to Carnforth (WCRC) before continuing to York where it was immediately withdrawn for overhaul.

The overhaul of 4472 *Flying Scotsman* took longer than expected due to the need to make good the ravages of both time and poor workmanship over the years. The overhaul was finally completed in January 2016 and, following 'shakedown' running on the East Lancashire Railway, the locomotive was sent to Carnforth in February 2016 to undergo its loaded test run on the Carnforth Circuit.

Left: 4472 *Flying Scotsman* bears LNER WWII Unlined Black livery, smokebox BR fleet number and cab-side first LNER fleet renumbering as it passes Clitheroe on 4 February 2016 with its loaded test train.

Below Left: Having gained its main line certification, only two days later on 6 February 2016, 4472 *Flying Scotsman* curves through Greenholme with the Carnforth–Carlisle leg of a railtour from Euston to Carlisle, displaying its second LNER renumbering on its other cab-side.

Below Right: Restored to final BR condition as 60103 *Flying Scotsman*, the locomotive began a programme of heritage line visits and main line railtours in 2016. On 15 May 2016 60103 *Flying Scotsman* worked the Crewe–Holyhead and Holyhead–Crewe legs of a charter from Euston to Holyhead; the return leg is seen at Ffynnongroyw adjacent to the Dee Estuary.

PEPPERCORN 'A1' CLASS 4-6-2
BR = 60113–60162; 60163

This class was introduced in 1945 when Edward Thompson rebuilt original Gresley 'A1' Class 4-6-2 4470 *Great Northern* as a precursor to designing his own range of locomotives. He retired in 1946 and was succeeded by A.H. Peppercorn who redesigned the conversion to more Gresley standards and ordered forty-nine locomotives to the new design. All the locomotives were withdrawn and scrapped in the 1960s but, in the 1990s, a group of enthusiasts formed the A1 Steam Locomotive Trust (A1SLT) to recreate a locomotive to Peppercorn's design; work began in 1994 and in August 2008 the locomotive, numbered 60163, appeared at the Darlington base of the A1 Society.

Right: 60163 *Tornado* stands at Carlisle on 24 June 2010 awaiting time after an early arrival with THE CALEDONIAN TORNADO railtour returning from Glasgow Central to Crewe.

Below: 60163 *Tornado* curves through the closed Rimington station on 14 April 2010 whilst working a railtour returning from Carlisle to Crewe.

60163 *Tornado* curves through Greenholme on 22 September 2011 whilst ascending Shap with the Crewe–Carlisle leg of a Euston–Carlisle railtour.

PEPPERCORN 'A2' CLASS 4-6-2
BR = 60500–60539

This class was initiated by Edward Thompson in 1943 by the rebuilding of Gresley's six 'P2' Class 2-8-2 to a 4-6-2 configuration, following which he produced a further two variants of the design. He retired in 1946 and was replaced by A.H. Peppercorn who designed a further variant reverting to more Gresley principles of which 60532 *Blue Peter* was one of the fifteen locomotives (60525–60539) built to the latter design.

The locomotive was sold into preservation when withdrawn from BR service in 1966 but, as at December 2016, it is stored at the Crewe workshops of Jeremy Hosking's organisation awaiting overhaul and return to main line operation.

Right: 60532 *Blue Peter* curves into Shotlock Tunnel on 8 August 1992 with the northbound CUMBRIAN MOUNTAIN EXPRESS railtour from Kings Cross to Carlisle.

Below: 60532 *Blue Peter* is 'panned' on its approach to the summit at Ais Gill on 21 March 1992 with the southbound CUMBRIAN MOUNTAIN EXPRESS returning from Carlisle to Kings Cross.

GRESLEY 'V2' CLASS 2-6-2
BR = 60800–60984

This class was introduced by Sir Nigel Gresley in 1936 as a mixed traffic design that quickly proved to be a powerful locomotive for passenger use. Class doyen 60800 *Green Arrow* entered preservation when withdrawn from BR service in August 1962 and became part of the National Collection in 1971. It was subsequently transferred to the NRM when it relocated to York where, as at December 2016, it remains as a static exhibit following its withdrawal from main line service.

Top Right: 60800 *Green Arrow*, bearing LNER Lined Apple Green livery and fleet number, nears Ais Gill summit on 30 September 1989 as it powers the Carlisle–Hellifield leg of a railtour returning from Carlisle to Euston.

Below Left: 60800 *Green Arrow*, bearing BR Lined Green livery and fleet number, climbs away from Settle Junction on 29 December 1999 with a railtour from Preston to Carlisle.

Below Right: 60800 *Green Arrow*, bearing LNER Lined Apple Green livery and fleet number, begins its climb to Longpreston from Settle Junction on 13 May 1989 as it powers the Carlisle–Hellifield leg of the CUMBRIAN MOUNTAIN EXPRESS railtour returning from Carlisle to Kings Cross.

THOMPSON 'B1' CLASS 4-6-0
BR = 61000–61409

This class was introduced in 1942 as a mixed traffic design; originally intended by Sir Nigel Gresley to be a development of his two 'V4' Class 2-6-2 prototypes, his early death allowed Edward Thompson to design a conventional 4-6-0 as part of his policy of 'standardisation'.

Only two class members entered preservation: 61264 was rescued from Barry Scrapyard in July 1976 and, as at December 2016, it is based on the North Yorkshire

Moors Railway where it has main line certification, whilst 61306 entered preservation when withdrawn from BR service in 1967. 61306 was named *Mayflower* and has passed through a number of owners but, as at December 2016, it is based on the North Norfolk Railway, from where it makes occasional visits to heritage lines and operates on main line railtours.

Above: 61264 has rear end insurance from WCRC Class 47/7 47746, on 10 January 2014, as it approaches Ramsgreave whilst undertaking its loaded test run on the Carnforth Circuit following overhaul.

Above Left: 61264 pilots Peppercorn 'K1' Class 2-6-0 62005 through the outskirts of Kendal on 4 June 2004 whilst taking stock from Carnforth (WCRC) to Fort William as a prelude to operating the seasonal JACOBITE service between Fort William and Mallaig.

Left: 61306 *Mayflower*, bearing LNER Lined Apple Green livery and BR fleet number, climbs through Longpreston on 2 May 2013 whilst undergoing its loaded test run on the Carnforth Circuit following overhaul.

GRESLEY 'K4' CLASS 2-6-0
BR = 61993–61996; 61998

This class was introduced in 1937 to work trains on the West Highland route between Glasgow and Mallaig; 61997 was rebuilt from its original 'K4' class 3-cylinder design to a 2-cylinder design in 1945 that was subsequently improved by A.H. Peppercorn to become the 'K1' class.

61994 entered preservation with Viscount Garnock when withdrawn from BR service in December 1961 but, following his early death in 1989, the locomotive was bought by John Cameron who, as at December 2016, keeps it in private sidings by Thornton from where it is used on main line railtours and visits to heritage lines.

Top Right: 61994 *The Great Marquess* powers through Eldroth on 8 March 2007 whilst undertaking a loaded test run on the Carnforth Circuit following overhaul.

Below Left: 61994 *The Great Marquess* curves through Oubeck on 15 August 2012 whilst leaving Lancaster with the seasonal THE FELLSMAN service operated between Lancaster and Carlisle via the Ribble Valley and Settle & Carlisle routes.

Below Right: 61994 *The Great Marquess* races through Brock on 22 September 2014 with the Carlisle–Preston leg of THE WEST HIGHLANDER railtour returning from Mallaig to Euston.

PEPPERCORN 'K1' CLASS 2-6-0
BR = 61997; 62001–62070

61997 was rebuilt by Edward Thompson in 1945 from Gresley's 'K4' Class to a 2-cylinder locomotive but, after his retirement in 1946, his successor was A.H. Peppercorn who improved the design further but following Gresley principles and ordered seventy locomotives to his design.

62005 was withdrawn from BR service in December 1967 and immediately went as stationery boiler to a local ICI plant from where it was bought in May 1969 to provide a spare boiler for 'K4' Class 2-6-0 61994. In the event the boiler was not required and the locomotive was donated to the nascent North Eastern Locomotive Preservation Group (NELPG) and transferred to the NELPG base at Thornaby in June 1972.

As at December 2016, the locomotive is based on the North Yorkshire Moors Railway from where it both visits heritage lines and operates on main line railtours.

Top Right: 62005, bearing BR livery and fleet number and temporarily named *Lord of the Isles*, climbs out of Settle on 4 May 2009 whilst powering the Hellifield–Carlisle leg of a Newcastle–York–Carlisle railtour.

Below Left: 62005, bearing BR livery and fleet number, curves away from Settle Junction on 20 July 2006 whilst working a loaded test train in top'n tail mode with Class 33/0 33025 on an early Carnforth Circuit operated in anti-clockwise direction.

Below Right: 62005, bearing LNER Lined Apple Green livery and fleet number, leaves Hellifield on 20 March 1983 with the Hellifield–Carlisle leg of a railtour from Kings Cross to Carlisle.

Section 5:
British Railways (BR)

When British Railways came into being on 1 January 1948, created by the Transport Act 1947, the previous post-Grouping companies became regions of the new body and the locomotive fleets added blocks of numbers as noted to their fleet numbers. In addition to these blocks, further blocks were allocated, covering 10000–19999 for diesel locomotives, 20000–29999 for electric locomotives and 70000–99999 for a new range of standard steam locomotives. This latter group was divided into three further blocks: 70000–79999 for tender locomotives, 80000–89999 for tank locomotives and 90000–99999 for freight locomotives.

A range of twelve designs was created, resulting in the production of 999 locomotives, but the introduction of the Modernisation Plan in 1954 halted further production as future motive power was geared to diesel and electric traction.

STANDARD CLASS 7 'BRITANNIA' 4-6-2
BR = 70000–70054

This class was designed at Derby and built at Crewe as an express passenger locomotive with first allocations to the ER, LMR and WR depots. Initial mechanical problems, especially with axle movement, were soon remedied and the locomotives proved popular in service. Once the diesel and electric traction began to be delivered the class was concentrated on LMR depots from where they were subsequently withdrawn from service, although two examples were preserved – 70000 *Britannia* and 70013 *Oliver Cromwell*.

Above: Class doyen 70000 *Britannia* received a lengthy overhaul at the beginning of the twenty-first century and was finally released to the main line on 9 November 2010 when it undertook a test run between Crewe and Warrington. The locomotive was supported by WCRC Class 47 47500 and the consist was noted passing Acton Bridge on its outward journey.

Below: 70000 *Britannia* was called for Royal duty on 24 January 2012 when it worked the Preston–Wakefield leg of a Royal Train carrying H.R.H. The Prince of Wales. Known to be a supporter of railways, it is thought he was on the footplate as the train breasted Copy Pit en route to Wakefield for the first stop of his tour.

Top Left: 70000 *Britannia* breasts Ais Gill summit on 10 March 2012 whilst working the Carlisle–Crewe leg of a railtour returning from Carlisle to Bristol.

Top Right: 70013 *Oliver Cromwell* breasts Hoghton Summit on 11 February 2012 whilst working the Preston–Carlisle leg of the CUMBRIAN MOUNTAIN EXPRESS from Euston to Carlisle.

Below Right: 70013 *Oliver Cromwell* starts away from Preston on 23 April 2010 after making a stop for water whilst working a railtour returning from Edinburgh to Manchester Victoria.

STANDARD CLASS 8 'DUKE' 4-6-2
BR = 71000

This locomotive was built in 1954 to replace 'Princess Royal' Class 4-6-2 46202 *Princess Anne* which had been destroyed in the Harrow crash of October 1952. The locomotive was built at Crewe to a design by J.F. Harrison, then BR CME, who had been an LNER 'Premium Apprentice' under Sir Nigel Gresley, hence why, whilst built by an LMR workshops, it contains many LNER practices.

In practice it proved a diffident steamer and was an early withdrawal from BR service in 1962, but was sent to Barry for scrapping where it languished until bought for preservation and restoration in 1974. Unable to obtain BR drawings the preservation group calculated the locomotive's measurements, during which time it identified – and corrected – the cause of the poor steaming before returning the locomotive to main line service.

As at December 2016 the locomotive is undergoing overhaul at Jeremy Hosking's Crewe base with an anticipated return to main line operations.

71000 *Duke of Gloucester* **shows its power as it curves through Greenholme on 10 September 2004 whilst ascending Shap with the Carlisle–Crewe leg of a railtour from Euston to Carlisle.**

Cumbrian Visitor

Right: 71000 *Duke of Gloucester* curves past Siddick Wind Farm on 3 July 2010 as it accelerates a Crewe–Carlisle railtour from a water stop at Workington.

Below: 71000 *Duke of Gloucester* coasts through Bay Horse on 27 August 2005 with a railtour returning from Carlisle to Crewe.

71000 *Duke of Gloucester* accelerates away from a water stop at Workington on 24 February 2007 whilst working a Manchester Victoria–Carlisle railtour.

STANDARD CLASS 4 4-6-0
BR = 75000–75079

This class was designed by Brighton, with assistance from Derby, Doncaster and Swindon, and built at Swindon to work mixed traffic services over secondary lines. Locomotives were first allocated to depots on the LMR (45) and WR (20) with the final 15 being allocated to SR depots with modified tenders. Six class members have been preserved but, as at December 2016, none have main line certification.

75014 had a short spell of main line service before being sold to the Paignton & Dartmouth Railway where, as at December 2016, it operates on a private commercial line. On 15 June 2000 it was on main line duty as it left Carnforth for Fort William, piloting Class 31 31190 *Gryphon*, with the stock of the seasonal JACOBITE (Fort William–Mallaig) service heading northwards as a prelude to the start of seasonal operations.

STANDARD CLASS 4 2-6-0
BR = 76000–76114

This class was designed at Doncaster, based on H.G. Ivatt's LMSR Class 4 2-6-0 design, and built by Doncaster (15), Derby and Horwich for light freight duties; initial allocations were to ER (15), LMR(15), NER (13), ScR (35) and SR (37). Only four locomotives have been preserved, of which only 76079 had main line certification although this was joined by 76084 in late 2016 as this album was being prepared.

Left: 76079 is normally operated in tandem with a second locomotive but, on 15 March 2008, it worked singly with THE COTTON MILL EXPRESS circular railtour routed from Manchester Victoria via Hellifield and Carnforth returning to Manchester Victoria; the railtour is seen passing Clitheroe on its outward journey to Carnforth.

Below: 76079 pilots Stanier Class 5 4-6-0 45407 *The Lancashire Fusilier* out of Settle on 21 December 2005 whilst working a railtour from Hellifield to Carlisle.

76079 is seen in more normal mode on 21 February 2004 as it pilots Bulleid 'Battle of Britain' Class 4-6-2 34067 *Tangmere* off Ribblehead Viaduct whilst working the Carlisle–Hellifield leg of a railtour returning from Carlisle to Bristol.

STANDARD CLASS 4 2-6-4T
BR = 80000–80154

This class was designed at Brighton, based on the Fairburn LMSR 2-6-4T design, for local passenger services whilst the Standard Class 4 4-6-0 was designed as the tender version for mixed traffic duty. 155 locomotives were built, shared between Brighton (130), Derby (15) and Doncaster (10) with initial allocations to all regions except the WR. While fifteen locomotives were preserved, as at December 2016 none have main line certification hence are confined to operating on heritage lines.

In 1993, BR elected to train more crews on steam locomotives and arranged to hire locomotives and stock to operate a series of training runs between Carlisle and Kirkby Stephen for the purpose. On 5 March 1993 80080 curves past Armathwaite with a Carlisle to Kirkby Stephen training run during the period of operation.

STANDARD CLASS 9 2-10-0
BR = 92000–92250

This class was designed between Brighton and Derby for heavy freight duties with construction shared between Crewe (178) and Swindon (73) and allocations to the ER (85), LMR (100), NER(10) and WR (56). The original intent was to design a 2-8-2 but this was altered to 2-10-0, based on Riddles' experience with that wheel arrangement during Second World War railway service. Nine locomotives have been preserved but the interface with modern trackwork means that, as at December 2016, all examples are confined to operating on heritage lines.

92220 *Evening Star* was named to commemorate it being the last steam locomotive to be built by BR when completed at Swindon in August 1960; it entered preservation as part of the National Collection when withdrawn from BR service and moved to York when the National Rail Museum relocated there during 1977. On 23 April 1984 92220 *Evening Star* made several runpasts over Ribblehead Viaduct whilst working the Carlisle–Hellifield leg of the southbound CUMBRIAN MOUNTAIN EXPRESS railtour returning from Carlisle to Kings Cross.